THE LORD IS

INSPIRATION AND COM

BY

JOY CHRISTIAN

PUBLISHED BY

KRATOS PUBLISHERS

WITH INDEPENDENT PUBLISHING NETWORK

THE LORD IS MY SHEPHERD

Inspiration and Comfort for Your Soul

All bible Scripture quotations are from https://www.bible.com and unless otherwise indicated, are taken from the New King James Version.

ISBN: 978-1-78926-087-8

PUBLISHED BY
KRATOS PUBLISHERS
With independent publishing network

TABLE OF CONTENTS

DEDICATION

I dedicate this book to the Good Shepherd, my Lord and Saviour, Jesus Christ.

I also dedicate this book to my late parents, my mum Emlyn and my dad Aston, who were the ones who inspired me to read psalm 23 as a teenager.

ACKNOWLEDGEMENTS

My deepest appreciation goes to my whole family, my brothers and sisters, nieces, nephews and cousins and to my spiritual mother, Mrs Renee, who always encourages me to pray.

I also say a big thank you to all the pastors that have encouraged me to write this book.

1

THE LORD IS MY SHEPERD

The Lord is my Shepherd

The 23rd Psalm is reputed as a psalm of David and helps us to see God (Father, Spirit, Jesus Christ) in the light of what He does for us. Through the experience of David who was a shepherd and who was very aware of What a Shepherd does for the sheep. The word Shepherd signifies caretaker, protector, provider, companion, faithfulness and security.

The Lord is **my** Shepherd signifies a personal relationship because the good Shepherd knows each of His sheep by name and also knows the different personality and temperament of each sheep. This is a different kind of Shepherd... not an ordinary one. He is one who actually created every one of those He is looking after and therefore knows each individually.

Psalm 139:1,2 says:
O Lord, you have searched me and known me, you know my sitting down and my rising up; you understand my thought afar off.

Psalms 139: 13 also says:
For you formed my inward parts;
You covered me in my mother's womb.

In return, the sheep is overwhelmed by its Shepherd's kindness in this personal relationship and learns to trust its shepherd.

My Sheep Hear my voice and I know them, and they follow me: and I give unto them eternal life and the shall never perish neither shall any man pluck them out of my hand.

John 10:27,28

The Lord is **my** shepherd also signifies ownership and therefore entitlement , such as in a child to parent relationship. No Wonder Jesus taught us to pray.......

"**Our** Father in heaven....."

Psalm 91:2 declares God our Protector:

*I will say of the Lord, He is **my** refuge and **my** fortress: **my** God; in Him will I trust.*

God is our light and our salvation. We can rely on Him. He is the Light in dark times or situations. I think About the many times God rescued me and brought me out of the dark valley.

The Lord is my light and salvation.

Whom Shall I fear?
The Lord is the strength of my life;
Of whom Shall I be afraid?

Psalms 27:1

I don't know what your own dark time could have been but I remember a dark time when I was a little girl of just about 5 years of age. It was a period when I had to endure the humiliation from an infant school teacher who kept shouting at me in front of the whole school because I was not able to pronounce the word "Frankincense" during rehearsals. The teacher had drafted me in to act as one of the three wise men in a Christmas play.

I had been a nervous and shy little girl and the teacher insisted I play the part while she screamed at me for not being able to pronounce the word properly. Rehearsals did not help me to perform better as I only got worse because of the constant criticism and I did not want to go to school. I was so sad and fearful that I cried so much but my tears did not change the teacher's attitude until rescue came in the form of another little girl who offered to swap roles with me and teacher agree. I remember what great relief I felt as a little girl. It was like light of all of a sudden shining through the darkness. Now I know it was God. No wonder psalmist said in verse 4 of the same psalm:

One thing I have desired of the Lord
that will I seek:
that I may dwell in the house of the Lord.
All the days of my life,   to
behold the beauty of the Lord,
and to inquire in His temple

Psalm 27:4

God has been very interested in each of us from baby hood before. He has His hand upon us to guide to protect and to lead us into a personal relationship with Him if we will yield to His promptings.

Sometimes, challenges make us doubt God when we focus more on those Challenges.

Jesus said to him, "Thomas, because you have seen me, you have believed. Blessed are those who have not seen and yet believe."

John 20:29

We need to focus more on God and get into His word so that we can build our faith in God.

2

I SHALL NOT WANT

The Lord is my Shepherd; I shall not be in want of any good thing.

I shall not lack any good thing. Why would the psalmist say this so confidently? As we noted earlier, the word shepherd signifies caretaker, protector, provider, companion, faithfulness and security.

There are many shepherds, but when the one that takes Care of you is the creator of the universe, then you know that there is abundance. More than enough for the every Sheep.

After all, He is the creator of all. When the creator Himself, for Whatever reason, s besotted with you enough to die for you in the person of His son, Jesus Christ, to remove your sins from you and to redeem you to himself and make you His, you know there is nothing that you need that He does not want to give you.

What then shall we say to these things? If God is for us, who can be against us? He who did not spare His Own Son, but delivered Him up for us all, how shall He not with Him also freely give us all things?

Romans 8:31 -32

Jesus Christ said:

I am the good Shepherd: the good Shepherd giveth his life for the Sheep

John 10:11 KJV

Jesus Christ laid His life down for us that we might come into all that God has for us. That we might have all the good things God wants us to have. It was even for our justification that He rose up from the dead on the third day

Who was delivered for our offences and was raided again for our justification.

Romans 4:25 KJV

God is not broke. There is no lack in His kingdom. Rather than have shortage, he would just create more.

3

GREEN PASTURES AND STILL WATERS

He makes me to lie down in green pastures; He leads me beside the still waters

What do sheep need to stay healthy and strong? Green grass... luscious green grass and cool water. Sheep thrive on thesis. God knows exactly what you need personally. The good shepherd does not give you just what you need to survive but He also gives you all that you need as an individual to thrive.

God is your source and He is not cheap. The good shepherd does not just take the seep to where the grass is dry and withered. No he finds luscious green grass, excellent nutrition; good to the taste and soft enough to lie in .see God wants you to take a rest. Rest from anxiety and from anxious thoughts, rest from worry, rest from lack, rest from fear, rest from negative emotions and from those things that don't produce the best in you. That's why Jesus encourages us to:

Come unto me all ye that labour and are heavy laden, and I will give you rest.

Take my yoke upon you, and learn of me; for I am meek and lowly in heart and ye shall find rest unto your souls, for my yoke is easy and burden is light.

Matthew 11:28- 30 KJV

I remember my younger days when I could not hold on to a job due to poor self-esteem. It was difficult as I was inconstant lack. I had become a Christian and so I began to ask God for help. I Trusted in His promises and I began to fast and pray. He answered me and delivered me from poor self-esteem and since then, keeping a job has not been a problem.

As we follow the good shepherd, our creator, our God , our Saviour Jesus Christ, He will lead us to all good things and abundance of blessings. He leads, teaches and instructs us in the way that we should take. He offers us direction He leads us beside the still, quiet waters, Quiet waters signify peaceful and calm. God quenches our thirsts physically, emotionally and spiritually. He fills us with his Holy Spirit, that fountain of life, with the Holy Spirit in us, He leads and guides us by His peace. In a lot of matters, the Holy Spirit will also give us a sense of peace about whatever way He wants us to take or whatever He wants us to do (even if circumstances suggest otherwise) and He withdraws that sense of peace about whatever it is that He does not want us to do or say.

In the last day, that great day of the feast, Jesus Stood and Cried saying if any man thirst, let him come unto me, and drink He that believeth on me as the scripture hath said out of his belly shall flow rivers of living water. (But this spake he of the Spirit, which they that believe on him should receive: for the Holy Ghost was not yet given; because that Jesus was not yet glorified.)

The sheep of His pasture must be led by His Holy Spirit He wants to lead us in quiet confidence:

" woe to the rebellious children," says the Lord, "who take counsel, but not of Me, and who devise plans, but no of My Spirit, that they may add sin to sin; who walk to go down to Egypt, and have not asked my Advice…"

For thus says the Lord God, the Holy One of Israel: "In returning and res you shall be saved; in quietness and confidence shall be your strength…."

Isaiah 30:1,2,15

GOD RESTORES ME

He restores my soul; He leads me in the path of righteousness for His name's sake.

God does not only take care of our physical material needs but also our emotional and spiritual needs, He restores our souls, not just with physical nourishment and replenishment but He meets our soulish and spiritual needs with the bread of His word and with satisfaction and replenishment that only the Holy Spirit gives.

> *In the last day, that great day of the feast, Jesus Stood and Cried saying if any man thirst, let him come unto me, and drink He that believeth on me as the scripture hath said out of his belly shall flow rivers of living water.*
> *(But this spake he of the Spirit, which they that believe on him should receive: for the Holy Ghost was not yet given; because that Jesus was not yet glorified.)*
> **John 7:37-39 KJV**

With the love and acceptance He bestows upon us, He heals our souls. By His presence in our lives and by us having a personal relationship with him, He satisfies the deep longing of a human heart for love, acceptance and self-actualisation.

Also, we are His ambassadors. We reflect His glory, he has a name and reputation to protect, therefore He takes utmost care of us and He leads us so we can be righteous before Him, according to His wisdom, according to His word.

He knew that we could not fulfil the righteous requirement of His law by ourselves alone and so He gave Jesus Christ as propitiation for our sins. He has redeemed us by the power that is in the blood of Jesus Christ, so that sin shall not have dominion over us because we are now under grace. He gave us the gift of righteousness through the blood of Jesus Christ. That is, when Jesus Christ becomes the Shepherd, the Bishop of our soul, your saviour, you then inherit righteousness that is a gift from God. Righteousness is imputed unto us through Jesus Christ who never committed any sin and He also begins to lead us and empower us by His Holy Spirit to do the right thing and to be obedient to Him. We then enjoy all of the blessings that God so graciously wants to bestow upon us.

5

VICTORY OVER THE VALLEY OF THE SHADOW OF DEATH

Yea, though I walk through the valley of the shadow of death, I will fear no evil; for you are with me; your rod and your staff, they comfort me.

The valley of the shadow of death.... Danger, evil, darkness, or simply a situation that seems hopeless, when there seems to be no light at the end of the tunnel! Even during such a time, God is present and darkness is like daylight to Him, the psalmist declares that there's nothing to fear because of the reassuring presence of the Good Shepherd.

I will say of the LORD, "He is my refuge and my fortress; My God, in Him I will trust." Surely He shall deliver you from the snare of the fowler and from the perilous pestilence. He shall cover you with His feathers, And under His wings you shall take refuge; His truth shall be your shield and buckler. You shall not be afraid of the terror by night, nor of the arrow that flies by day, Nor of the pestilence that walks in darkness, Nor of the destruction that lays waste at noonday.

Psalm 91:2-6

A favourite story of mine is about a certain old lady who had just become a Christian when her car was hijacked and stolen with her inside the car. He two male villains bundled her into backseats of the car and drove off. Shocked, she could not even remember any verse in psalm 91 clearly. Nothing seemed to come out of her mouth when she tried to pray the above verses of scripture so she cried "Feathers!" "Feathers!" "Feathers!" To everyone's surprise, feathers appeared from nowhere and began to fill the car until the two villains parked the car and ran off what a great deliverance!

God is our protector. He delivers us from all evil. He is the good shepherd who is always present with us. His rod and staff comforts us. A shepherd's rod and staff are used to guide, to protect and to offer direction. God's word (God's truth) shields us, gives us guidance, protection and direction. It is also for our defence and for attacking and defeating the enemy. His truth is indeed our shield and our buckler.

God's rod and staff comfort us. Jesus said that the Holy Spirit is our comforter because He will teach us all things, bring all things to our remembrance, guide us and direct us.

And I will pray the Father, and he shall give you another comforter, that he may abide with you forever; Even the Spirit of truth; whom The world

26

cannot receive, because it seeth him not neither knoweth him: but ye know him; for He dwelleth with you, and shall be in you. I will not leave you comfortless: I will come to you

John 14:16-18(KJV)

But the comforter, which is the Holy Ghost , whom the Father will send in my name, he shall teach you all things, and bring all things to your remembrance, whatsoever I have said unto you.

John 14:26 (KJV)

The Holy Spirit and God's word give us peace. The reassuring, protecting, comforting and delivering presence and power of God ensures that the dark valley is nothing but a 'walk through' that never becomes permanent.

6

A BANQUET FOR ME

You prepare a table before me in the presence of my enemies; you anoint my head with oil; my cup runs over.

God cares for us so much that He throws a party for us, even in the presence of our enemies. He delights in giving us all the good things that enemies don't want us to have. In His graciousness, He gives us those good things that enemies don't think we deserve.

> *He delivers me from my enemies. You also life me up above those who rise against me;...*

Psalm 18:48

God throwing us a party, anointing our heads and blessing us in the presence of our enemies, shows our enemies that contrary to what they would like to believe about us, we are approved, we are accepted and not rejected, we are preferred, we are chosen. This is a cure for hurting emotions, if we will look unto God and trust in him rather than fretting. Cheer up child of God. Are you going through any difficulty at the moment? No matter how difficult it seems. Just hold on because God is about to throw a party. Even if the problem was your fault, so far you have now repented; he will soon prepare a table

before you in the presence of your enemies. Just like He did for the prodigal son. He won't leave your loved ones out. He'll invite them too so they can rejoice with you. And if He could do this for the prodigal son who had sinned, how much more for a faithful child of God ? Listen to what He said to the prodigal son's brother who had been faithful." All I have is yours"

"But he was angry and would not go in. therefore his father came out and pleaded with him.

"And He said to him, Son you are always with me and all that I have is yours

Luke 15:28,31

God's anointing oil upon our heads is Holy Spirit anointing. It is for honouring, for favoured selection, for approval. It is empowerment, it is enablement for office or task, it is endowment of skill or ability. It is empowerment to prosper. It is empowerment to be victorious. Our cup runs over with this blessing, this anointing, this enablement this empowerment, this prosperity. There is abundance, there is plenteousness. The Lord is my Shepherd; I do not lack any good thing.

7

GOD'S GOODNESS AND MERCY FOLLOW ME

Surely goodness and mercy shall follow me all the days of my life: and I will dwell in the house of the Lord forever.

Psalms 91 verse 1 tells us that he who dwells in the secret place of the most high shall abide under the shadow of the Almighty.

I will forever remain grateful for a miracle of protection one morning in the year 2007. It was very early in the morning as I got ready to go out. Before leaving home, I felt an urge to pray psalm 91 out aloud. I ignored the urge and continued to get ready. It became stronger until I burst out loudly declaring psalm 91 for myself. I finished dressing up and went out. I waited at the bus stop for a while and got on the bus when it arrived. I noticed a man also got on the bus with me. I went to sit upstairs on the double decker bus and so did the man who got on the bus with me. We met only one young man already sitting there and chatting away on his phone. I Sat in front of the young man with the phone and the man who came on the bus with me sat beside me. I wondered why he sat next to me when there were empty seats everywhere on the bus.

The young man on the phone ended his phone conversation and started pulling my hair and from behind. I moved uneasily in my sit and turned back and said do you mind? He stared at me like he hadn't done anything and then pulled my hair again. I shouted "stop it!" I began to get up to get off the bus as the bus was nearing my stop anyway. To my horror, he got up as well and pulled out a gun half hidden and said" get off" the bus!" Shocked I walked downstairs and got off at the bus stop which happened to be my stop. Another horrifying moment was when I realised he was getting off too. Coming to stand beside me. I stood still shocked, but I had heard the Lord say "don't move or go anywhere". Then I saw the man who entered the bus with me getting off the bus too. I had never been so happy to see someone get off the bus. He came and stood beside me on the other side. He brought out his phone as if to make a phone call and the dangerous guy with the gun ran away I heaved a sigh of relief, thanking my knight in shining armour for coming to my aid. He told me his name is David as we walked away from the bus stop and that he had been listening to the dangerous guy's phone conversation while we were on the bus and had heard him talking about killing a particular person. I thanked David profusely until he went on his way. I was so glad for such Godly protection and deliverance. Was David an angel? Probably. Was I glad I had finally yielded to that urge to pray psalm 91 that morning before leaving home? You bet!

I had a similar great deliverance one morning in 2008, as a car driving at top speed was able to screech to a halt just on time to avoid hitting me!

Always remember that God is indeed your shepherd. No matter what the situation, just turn it all over to God who is able to rescue you in any difficult situation. God is always with us by His Holy Spirit. the same Holy Spirit that was there at creation and at your conception is your comforter, your counsellor and teacher if you are a child of God. Your comforter is someone called alongside you to help you. So turn over your life reins to Him. He is with you to help you in every situation.

It is the Holy Spirit that empowers us to live victoriously in Christ Jesus and to shun unrighteousness as God requires of us.

Because it is written "Be holy, for I am holy."
1Peter 1:16

For example, you might be advanced in years and still single. You would like to get married but are still single though you have asked God in prayer countless times. And are committed to living a holy life as God required. Remember that it is the Holy Spirit that enables you to live holy. He helps you get rid of strife, anger, jealousy, sexual sin and all other unrighteousness. God is faithful and His Holy Spirit abides in you and with you and helps you to fulfil your own part of the covenant you have with God, and God who always keeps His promises will also keep His own part. God will always keep His promises so keep your focus on Him. He will be with you in times of trouble and cover you in His pavilions to protect you. He that dwells in the secret place of the Most high is guaranteed God's protection. Hallelujah, glory be to God!

> *He who dwells in the secret place of the Most High Shall abide under the shadow of the Almighty. I will say of the LORD, "He is my refuge and my fortress; My God, in Him I will trust." Surely He shall deliver you from the snare of the fowler and from the perilous pestilence. He shall cover you with His feathers, and under His wings you shall take refuge; His truth shall be your shield and buckler. You shall not be afraid of the terror by night, nor of the arrow that flies by day, nor of the pestilence that walks in darkness, Nor of the destruction that lays waste at noonday. A thousand may fall at your side and ten thousand at your right hand; but it shall not come near you*
> **Psalm 91:1 – 7**

As you continue to get closer to God, seeking His face He will draw closer to you as well. You will begin to discover your gifts and abilities and your purpose in life. As a little girl I was nervous and shy, hardly able to speak in public. Today, God has helped me so much and equipped me that I speak publicly as an evangelist. In Christ Jesus, weakness can very much turn to strength. It is god who enables and empowers us. There are examples of characters in the bile who overcame weaknesses and obstacles to achieve their purpose in life. My favourite characters are Moses and Joseph, who overcame all obstacles and achieved their purpose. I encourage you to study the Bible. You will learn a lot from studying Bible Characters.

God's protection, favour, kindness and love follow me always because I Abide with the Good Shepherd and His Presence always brings me his favour, loving-kindness and mercy. I am excited about dwelling in God's house and presence forever. I am excited about hanging out with Him all the days of my life, forever. Being in His presence and worshipping Him brings down the glory of God. In God's presence. We are covered by His anointing and darkness dispelled, the enemy is defeated. Hanging out with God and being in His presence causes His anointing to be upon us. His power rubs off on us. I Choose to dwell in God's presence and in the secret place of the Most high through prayer, reading the Bible praising and worshipping God, Going to church regularly and serving God and so I Abide under the shadow of the Almighty. He satisfies me with long life and shows me His salvation always. I enjoy all round salvation, God's favour, goodness, kindness, love all the days of my life.

SALVATION PRAYER

That if thou shalt confess with thy mouth the Lord Jesus, and shalt believe in thine heart that God hath raised him from the dead, thou shalt be saved. For with the heart man believeth unto righteousness and with the mouth confession is made unto salvation

Romans 10:9,19 (KJV)

Pray this prayer

Almighty God, I am sorry for all my sins, I ask you to forgive me. I believe that Jesus Christ is the Son of God and that He died to save me from my sins. I believe that God raised Him from the dead. I confess Jesus Christ and receive him as my Lord and saviour.

For he has rescued us and has drawn us to Himself from the dominion of darkness, and has transferred us to the kingdom of His beloved Son, in whom we have redemption (because of His sacrifice, resulting in) the forgiveness of our sins (and in the cancellation of sin's penalty).

Colossians 1:13,14 (AMP)